THE GLORY OF GURUVAYURAPPAN

AND THE MIRACLES OF GURUVAYUR

K C R RAJA

Copyright © K C R Raja
All Rights Reserved.

This book has been self-published with all reasonable efforts taken to make the material error-free by the author. No part of this book shall be used, reproduced in any manner whatsoever without written permission from the author, except in the case of brief quotations embodied in critical articles and reviews.

The Author of this book is solely responsible and liable for its content including but not limited to the views, representations, descriptions, statements, information, opinions and references ["Content"]. The Content of this book shall not constitute or be construed or deemed to reflect the opinion or expression of the Publisher or Editor. Neither the Publisher nor Editor endorse or approve the Content of this book or guarantee the reliability, accuracy or completeness of the Content published herein and do not make any representations or warranties of any kind, express or implied, including but not limited to the implied warranties of merchantability, fitness for a particular purpose. The Publisher and Editor shall not be liable whatsoever for any errors, omissions, whether such errors or omissions result from negligence, accident, or any other cause or claims for loss or damages of any kind, including without limitation, indirect or consequential loss or damage arising out of use, inability to use, or about the reliability, accuracy or sufficiency of the information contained in this book.

Made with ❤ on the Notion Press Platform
www.notionpress.com

Contents

1. Origin: Puranic Legends   1
2. Into Modern History   5
3. Melpathur Narayana Bhattathiri   8
4. Chapter 4   13
5. Chapter 5   17
6. Kururamma   22
7. Chembai Vaidyanatha Bhagavathar   25
8. Chapter 8   29
9. Chapter 9   35

I

ORIGIN: Puranic Legends

ORIGIN: PURANIC LEGENDS

The story, according to Hindu belief, goes back to the period of creation by Brahma, the beginning of Padmakalpa. Vishnu appeared before Brahma and when Brahma wished to get moksha without the bondage of births, rebirths and karma, Vishnu presented an idol of himself and asked him to worship it. Brahma did this for a long time and then in the 'Varaha kalpa' gave it to the sage Sutapa and his wife Prsni who were longing for a child. They worshipped the idol and prayed for a son. In response to their prayers, Lord Vishnu appeared before them and said that he himself will be born as their child in three successive births; and in each they would be able to worship the idol given to them.

The first birth of Vishnu was as Prsnigarbha, the son of Sutapa and Prsni in the Satya yuga, the second as Vamana in Tretayuga when Sutapa and Prsni were born as

Kashyapa and Aditi and the third as Lord Krishna in Dwapara yuga, when Sutapa and Prsni were born as Vasudeva and Devaki. In all three births they worshipped the idol God had given them.

Although he himself was an avatar of Lord Vishnu, Krishna took the idol with him, worshipped it and took it to Dwaraka, his new abode and built a temple for the idol.. Finally the Dwapara Yuga came to an end. Before leaving for Vaikunta, Krishna called his friend and disciple, Udhava. He told him that the Dwapara yuga was coming to an end, that Dwaraka would be destroyed and that the lone survivor would be the idol that his parents, in their three births, and he had been worshipping. Krishna wanted Udhava to hand the idol to sage Brihaspati, considered Guru by the devas. Udhava had already left Dwaraka but before leaving sent a message to Brihaspati. By the time Brihaspati arrived, the deluge had materialised. Brihaspati saw the idol floating on the high seas but could not go anywhere near it. He called upon Vayu the god of the Winds, one of his disciples and Vayu with the help of Varun, the lord of the oceans and water, to bring the idol to the shore. They didn't know where to install the idol. Suddenly Parashurama appeared and told them to install it in Bhargava Kshetra, the land he had created with his axe. (Kerala).

Brihaspati and Vayu carried the idol and travelled through the sky to find an appropriate place on the shores of Bhargava Kshetra. They spotted and hovered around a beautiful piece of land with a lake, and lush greenery, which spread at once an atmosphere of peace and friendliness. There seemed to be something divine about the place. They then saw Shiva and Parvati dancing near that lake. They prostrated before Shiva who had been waiting for this to happen. Shiva pointed to the place where they were standing and said that was itself the ideal place for the installation of the idol.

Shiva then said that since the idol has been brought and is to be installed by Guru(Brihaspati) and Vayu, the place would be called Guruvayur.

Brihaspati then got the divine architect, Vishwakarma to erect a temple for the deity. Brihaspati and Vayu installed the idol. Shiva performed the first Pooja . The devas headed by Indra showered flowers and sage Narmada sang in praise of the Lord. The deity came to be known as Guruvayurappan, the God or Lord of Guruvayur. It is believed that Vishnu is ever present here as he is in Vaikunta and hence Guruvayur is referred to as Bhuloka Vaikunta.

The place Lord Shiva preferred for himself and Parvathy was called Mahimayur, now known as Mammiyur.

The story of Guruvayur takes us back to ' Gurupavanapuresa Mahatymam' in Narada Purana. King Parikshit(grandson of Arjuna and son of Abhimanyu) suffered from a curse and died of a snake bite from the snake king Takshaka. Parikshit's son, Janamejaya sought to avenge the death of his father by killing all snakes including Takshaka and ventured on a yajna called 'Sarpahuti Yajna (snake sacrifice). This killed thousands of innocent snakes but Takshaka could not be killed because he had had Amrita, the nectar of immortality. Janamejaya was cursed by the snakes and contracted leprosy. He tried all cures but none worked. One day the sage Athreya visited him. The sage advised him to visit Guruvayur and worship Vishnu. He told him of the glory of Guruvayurappan. Janamejaya stayed for a year at Guruvayur to worship Guruvayurappan and also visited the Mammiyur temple to worship Lord

Shiva. One night while asleep, he felt the healing touch of Guruvayurappan. He was cured of the sickness. He went back, a happy man.

For centuries, men have flocked to Guruvayur to pray to the deity, the incarnation of Vishnu as a small boy. Their faith and devotion have only increased and been reinforced by their personal experiences of the power and compassion of Guruvayurappan. We all bow to him and chant his name. This book too is a chant, a prayer to Guruvayurappan.

Notes:

Yugas:

.1. Hindu scriptures talk of three main divisions of time: yuga, and Kalpa.There are four yugas as shown below:

Krita yuga 4800 divine years

Treta yuga 3600 divine years

Dwapara yuga 2400 divine years

Kali yuga 1200 divine years

Total (maha yuga) 12000 divine years

One year of the mortals equals one day of the gods. Therefore one maha yuga equals 12000x360=4.32 million years of mortals. It is said that a thousand such mahayugas constitute a day in the life of Brahma.

2. Brihaspati: Considered the master of sacred wisdom.sage counsellor of Indra in his wars against the asuras. Also known as Guru(Jupiter) a generous planet.

II
Into Modern History

INTO MODERN HISTORY

It is believed that the Guruvayur temple was constructed around the 14th century. The main shrine in Guruvayur dates back to antiquity. It is believed to have been rebuilt in 1638. By then the temple had already become the most popular pilgrimage centre in Kerala. Stories about great devotees and their blissful experiences had already become known in other parts of Kerala and beyond. They included even Shankaracharya and highlighted the work of persons like Melpathur Battathiripad, Poonthanam, Vilwamangalth Swami and Manavedan Raja.

The earliest records appear in the 17th century.

In 1716 the Dutch raided Guruvayur looted the treasures and set fire to the Western gopuram. This was rebuilt in 1747. In 1766 Haider Ali captured Kozhikode and then Guruvayur. He demanded a huge amount, 10000 fanams as ransom to spare the temple. The ransom was paid by Vatekkappat Varier. Pilgrims fled in fear. On a request from the Malabar Governor Srinivasa Rao, Haider Ali however granted a devadaya to save the temple. In 1789 Tipu Sultan invaded and set fire to the temple but it was saved by timely rain. The idol was taken and hidden underground in anticipation of Tipu's takeover. In 1789 Tipu was defeated by the British. The idol was then restored to the temple shrine and reinstalled on 17th September 1792.

From 1825 to 1900, Ullanad Panickers took care of the upkeep of the temple. Many renovations was done between 1859 and 1892 of the Chuttambalam, the Koottambalam, the Vilakkumatam and the Sasta Shrine. The roof also got copper sheeting during this period. The hours of worship were fixed in 1900 by the then Administrator of the temple, Kanti Menon. He was also instrumental in the installation of the big bell, streamlining administrative procedures and reconstructing the Pathayapura.

In 1928 the Zamorin once again took over the responsibility for administering the temple.

In 1931-32, the Congress leader and Gandhian, Kelappan launched a Satyagraha fast to protest against the ban in force on the entry of the "untouchables" into the temple. Although it did not produce immediate results, the Travancore Temple Entry proclamation of 1936 and public pressure led to similar measures in Malabar in 1946 and 1947. Since then, all Hindus have had access to the temple. The Namaskaram Sandhya reserved for Brahmins in the temple's Ootupera was stopped in the 1980s and from 1982 the Devaswom itself started feeding 500 to 1000 pilgrims every day.

On 30 th November 1970, a big fire broke out in the temple and raged for five hours; it gutted the

Chuttambalam, and the Vilakkumatamon in the west, north and south. Hindus, Muslims and Christians joined hands in putting it out. Almost miraculously the vigraha, sreekovil, and the shrines of Ayyappa, Ganesha and Bhagavathi remained unaffected.

In 1978-79, under the Guruvayur Devaswom Act 1978, a Guruvayur Devaswom Board was constituted with the responsibility to look after the Guruvayur temple and the ' subordinate' temples. The Act provided for a Commissioner to be in charge of the Committee and an Administrator appointed by the State Government to be the Chief Executive. The Zamorin would remain a member of the committee.

Since then, several steps have been taken from time to time to develop Guruvayur and make it pilgrim friendly. Apart from rail connection, easier access by road and facilities for lodging, the Central Government has announced plans to develop Guruvayur in a big way as a destination for temple tourism.

III

Melpathur Narayana Bhattathiri

Melpathur Narayana Bhattathiri

Nothing would perhaps be more fitting to the narration of the spiritual experiences of devotees than recalling the story of the devotee, Melpathur Narayana Bhattathiri. Bhattathiri was not merely an ardent devotee; he left for posterity a creation that has been sung by countless generations for more than four centuries. Narayaneeyam encapsulates Srimad Bhgvatha and describes beautifully the nine avatars of Vishnu. The story of how it came to be written and of the person, MELPATHUR who wrote it is a fascinating one.

Sri Narayana Bhattathiri (1560-1646), was born in MELPATHUR, a village near Thirunavaya on the banks of the river Bharathapuzha. He had his training in Sastras from his father, Matridatta(a great scholar), and went on to learn from the School of astronomy and mathematics founded by Madhava of Samgamagrama(Kerala School of Astronomy and Meathematics). He learnt Rig Veda from Madhava, tharka sastra (logic, reasoning or arguments) from Damodara and Vyakarana (grammar) from Achyuta Pisharady and became a pandit by the age of 16, Achyuta Pisharody became his guide and mentor. He married Pisharody's niece and settled in Trikandiyur.

Pisharoty was later struck by paralysis. Unable to see the suffering of his guru MELPATHUR used his yogic strength to take the disease on himself. This was his gurudakshina. Pisharoty was cured of the illness but no medicine could cure Narayana.Melpathur then decided to go to Guruvayur to seek permanent cure for his ailment. It is said that he left for Guruvayur on 19 Chinnam 761Malayalam Calendar which approximates to 3 September 1586. (at the age of 27).

The story goes that before going to Guruvayur, Melpathur went to Thunjath Ezuthachan a contemporary and one of the greatest-ever literary figures in Kerala(who had translated Ramayana into Malayalam) for advice on a cure. Ezuthachan's message was an incomprehensible three word reply' Meen thottu kootuka' (Start with the taste of fish!) An ordinary Brahmin would have thought it as enigmatic as insulting but the scholar and devotee in Melpathur interpreted it as advice to start from Vishnu's avatar in the form of a fish (matsyavatar). Bhattathiri started with matsyavar and covered the incarnations of Vishnu in his composition in praise of Narayana, Lord Guruvayurappa. The book came to be known as Narayaneeyam.

Narayaneeyam was composed in a series of dasakas (ten slokas), each das aka ending with a prayer to the Lord to cure him of his illness. Every day he sang 10 slokas and in 100 days he finished his composition. On 28 Vrischikam 762 Malayalam Calendar (correspond to 27 November 1586) he finished the last dasakam. On finishing this he was cured.

Melpathur went back to his illam a happy cured man. He lived till the age of 86 and produced several books, shifting to Kochi, Kozhikode and finally to Mookola in the present day Malappuram district where he lived for 20 years in the Devi temple. Returning from the temple one day he suddenly collapsed and died, as peacefully as he had also wished to die.

Narayaneeyam consists of 1044 slokas in Sanskrit. They give a summary of the 14000 verses of the Bhagavatha Purana. It portrays the complete life of Lord Krishna.

The 99th dasakam was an act of surrender at the feet of the Lord. Bhattadhiri wished to close the work with 1024 slokams since the sacred manthram of Gayathri mantra had 24 aksharas.

When he finished sloka 1023 Bhattathiri bowed in total surrender and thought of Shukracharya's blessing to King Parikshit with which the King had a Darshan of Vishnu in Vaikuntam. As he raised his head, he had a grand and glorious 'Vaikunta Darshan' of Guruvayurappan inside the sanctum sanctorum of the temple. And he started in the final dasakam the description of that experience with the sloka ' agre pasyami' ... I see before me..

(These three slokas and their meaning in English have been taken from the website

Narayaneeyam An Easy Access to the Great Stotra. The translation references the work of Swami Tapasyananda of Ramakrishna Math, Chennai and of Shri S N Sastry published by CCMT Mumbai)

अग्रे पश्यामि तेजो निबिडितरकलायावलीलोभनीयं
पीयूषाप्लावितोऽहं तदनु तदुदरे दिव्यकैशोरवेषम् ।
तारुण्यारम्भरम्यं परमसुखरसास्वादरोमाञ्चिताङ्गै-
रावीतं नारदाद्यैर्विलसदुपनिषत्सुन्दरीमण्डलैश्च ॥ १ ॥

In front of me, I see a bluish radiance excelling a very thick array of Kalaaya (blue lily) flowers. I am bathed in the nectar of the sight. Then, in the centre of the radiance, I see the form of a divine young body made enchanting by the budding of youth. He is surrounded by sages like Naarada thrilled with ecstatic bliss, and by a group of beautiful women who are the Upanishads embodied.

And Narayaneeyam ends with these three slokas :

मञ्जीरे मञ्जुनादैरिव पदभजनं श्रेय इत्यालपन्तं
पादाग्रं भ्रान्तमिज्जत्प्रणतजनमनोमन्दरोद्धारकूर्मम् ।
उत्तुङ्गाताम्रराजन्नखरहिमकरज्योत्स्नया चाश्रितानां
सन्तापध्वान्तहन्त्री ततिमिनकुलये मङ्गलामङ्गुलीनाम् ॥ ९ ॥

I meditate on Thy anklets with their sweet sound, which, as it were, sweetly confirm the excellence of worshipping at Thy feet. Thy incarnation of the tortoise which lifted the Mandaar mountain at the time of the deluge, Thy forefeet lift the minds of the people who prostrate at Thy feet. Thy toenails, of Thy auspicious toes, slightly raised, very red and shining are like the moonlight expelling the darkness of the sorrows of Thy devotees. I meditate on them.

योगीन्द्राणां त्वदङ्गेष्वधिकसुमधुरं मुक्तिभाजां निवासो
भक्तानां कामवर्षद्युतरुकिसलयं नाथ ते पादमूलम् ।
नित्यं चित्तस्थितं मे पवनपुरपते कृष्ण कारुण्यसिन्धो
हृत्वा निश्शेषतापान् प्रदिशतु परमानन्दसन्दोहलक्ष्मीम् ॥ १० ॥

O Lord! Among the parts of Thy body, the soles of Thy feet are the most beloved and coveted to the great yogis. The liberated ones reside there. They pour all the desires of their devotees and are like the sprouts of the celestial tree. O Lord of Guruvaayur! O Lord Krishna! may those feet always rest in my heart. O Ocean of Compassion! destroy all my sorrows and confer a full abundant flow of Supreme Bliss.

अज्ञात्वा ते महत्वं यदिह निगदितं विश्वनाथ क्षमेथाः
स्तोत्रं चैतत्सहस्रोत्तरमधिकतरं त्वत्प्रसादाय भूयात् ।
द्वेधा नारायणीयं श्रुतिषु च जनुषा स्तुत्यतावर्णनेन
स्फीतं लीलावतारैरिदमिह कुरुतामायुरारोग्यसौख्यम् ॥ ११ ॥

O Lord of the Universe! Deign to pardon me for what I have said here, not knowing fully Thy greatness. This hymn consists of more than a thousand verses. May it be the source of Thy abounding grace. It is in two ways Naaraayaneeyam. May this hymn which describes in accordance with the Vedas, Thy creative actions and Thy sportive incarnations, confer long life, good health and happiness.

Om NamO Bhagavate Vaasudevaaya|
Om NamO NaaraayaNaaya|
Om NamO NamaH ||

Notes:
Sources:
Wikiwand on Melpathur Narayana Bhattathiri.
Ramanuja.org
Narayaneeyam: An easy access to the Great Strotra-references: Shriman Narayaneeyam by S N Sastry published by CBMT, Mumbai and Narayaneeyam translated by Swami Tapasyananda, Sri Ramakrishna Math, Chennai.

IV

Poonthanam Nambudiri

Poonthanam Nambudiri (1547–1640AD) was a contemporary of Melpathur Bhattathiri. Twelve years older than Melpathur, Poonthanam too lived long to worship the Lord through his own poetical works. Melpathur was an erudite scholar, who channelled his Bhakti through Jnana; Poonthanam, one whose jnana was subordinated to his overpowering Bhakti. In Melpathur's works his knowledge of Vyakarana(grammar) shone through all the lines whereas Poonthanam's lines touched one's heart with their sense of reflective melancholy. Melpathur's was a work of Sanskrit scholarship; Poonthanam's one of ordinary Malayalam that anyone in Kerala would understand. Together they constituted two towering figures in the history of the Guruvayur temple.

Poonthanam was born in 1547 in a Nambudiri family in Keezhattoor, a village, near Perintalmanna, in present-day Malappuram District in Kerala. He married at the age of 20 but for many years the couple had no children. . He used to fervently recite Santanagopalam and perhaps in answer to this they had a son. Poonthanam was overjoyed.

He wished to have a grand Annaprasanam ceremony and invited all his friends. Most tragically, the child died an hour before the ceremony. Heartbroken Poonthanam went to Guruvayur to pray. He prayed with the Puranic story of Kumaraharanam. It is said that Guruvayurappan was so touched by his devotion that he came as a boy and lay in his lap for a moment and consoled him.

From then onwards, Poonthananam considered Lord Krishna as his son.

Poonthanam's life was then spent composing poems in praise of Lord Guruvayurappan. He produced a masterpiece ' Jnanapana'. In lucid Malayalam that the ordinary person could understand. He writes in Jnanappana "While little Krishna is dancing in our hearts, do we need little ones of our own?". (ഉണ്ണിക്കൃഷ്ണ?മനസ്സി?കളിക്കുമ്പോ?ഉണ്ണിക? മറ്റു വേണമോ മക്കളായി"

It is said that Poontanam took his Jnanapana to Melpathur and requested him to go through it, hoping for improvement and appreciation. Melpathur, a great Sanskrit scholar, declined to go through it. The Lord himself appreciated Poontanam's devotion; he made it clear that he preferred Poonthanam's Bhakti(devotion) to Melpathur's Vibhakti (grammar)

Jnanapana is rooted in the ordinary experiences of men this world. Devoid of rhetoric it brings home philosophically the transitory nature of life's enjoyments and experiences.It stresses japa or chanting and repetition of the Lord's various names as the way to salvation. At the end of every verse in Jnanapana occurs the Nama japa 'Krishna Krishna Mukunda Janardana'.

Poonthanam has written several stotras (hymns) in Malayalam in praise of Guruvayurappan, in addition to

Njanappana, including Ghanasangham, Anandanrittam and Noottettu Hari. But Njanappana was his masterpiece. Typical of the composition is the following:

ഇന്നലെയോളമെന്തെന്നറിഞ്ഞീലാ
ഇനി നാളെയുമെന്തെന്നറിഞ്ഞീലാ
ഇന്നിക്കണ്ട തടിക്കു വിനാശവു
മിന്ന നേരമെന്നേതുമാറിഞ്ഞീലാ

[Innale yolam enthannu arinjeela,
Ini naleyum enthannu atrinjeela,
Ini kanda thadikku vinasamum,
Inna nearm enatharenjeela]

We do not know what happened to us yesterday nor do we know what will happen tomorrow. We do not know when this body will perish or what will happen the next moment. (Why worry about the past or present over which we have no control? Think of Now. Act in the living present!)

കണ്ടു കണ്ടങ്ങിരിക്കും ജനങ്ങളെ
കണ്ടിലെല്ന്നു വരുത്തുന്നതും ഭവാ?
രണ്ടുനാലു ദിനം കൊണ്ടൊരുത്തനെ
തണ്ടിലേറ്റി നടത്തുന്നതും ഭവാ?

Kandu kandangirikkyum janangale
Kandillennu varuthunnathum bhavaan
Randu nalu dinam kondoruthane
Thandiletti natathunnathum bhavaan

Those whom we see or are with us every day , we may never see again, if you wish so, Oh God! In two or four days a perfectly healthy man may be taken to the funeral pyre, if you wish so, Oh God!

മാളികമുകമുകളേറിയ മന്നന്റെ
തോളി? മാറാപ്പു കേറ്റുന്നതും ഭവാ?

Malika mukaleriya mannante,
Tholil marappu kettunnathum Bhavaan

The king residing in a palace (malika) today may lose everything and be in the streets tomorrow carrying a dirty piece of cloth on his shoulders..

There are many more lines in simple almost conversational Malayalam that any reader would understand. These are impactful because we see them happening in everyday life and Poonthanam ascribes them to ye Lord Almighty. He believes that men should focus on the present, lead an ethical life and worship God because what happens to is tomorrow would invariably be the result of what we had done in the past.

The Poonthanam Illam is close to Angadipuram , which opens out to the Thirumandhamkunnu Bhagavathi temple. The illam has a temple where Bhagavathy is installed as also the idol of Krishna.

The Illam was later taken over by the Guruvayur Devaswom, and is now the Poonthanam memorial and museum.

Sources:

Guruvayur.com- commentary by Savitri Puram for slokas and their meaning.

The reader is advised to refer to the work of Dr Gopi Kottoor: Poonthanam's Hymns: The Fountain of God, published by Writers Workshop, Calcutta.

There is an excellent article, The Charms of Poonthanam Ilam by Arun Narayan

Writer, Indian National Trust for Art and Cultural Heritage (INTACH)Palakkad Chapter.

V

Manavedan Raja

Manavedan Raja from the Zamorin family (1585-1658) was an ardent devotee of the Lord. He lived in Guruvayur most of the time, even when he became the Zamorin, unlike his predecessors who had to live in Calicut to discharge their administrative duties and to exercise their land and sea power to protect the kingdom.

Manavedan was a Sanskrit scholar, a disciple of the famous scholar, Thiruvegapuzha Anayath Krishna Pisharody and Desamangalathu Varier. He was a contemporary of Melpathur Bhattathiri and was greatly influenced by him and by Vilwamangalath Swamiyar. He grew into a poetic genius.(Only two of his works have survived- Poorvabharatha Champu composed in 1643 and the immortal Krishnagiti composed in 1654.)

Manavedan was the Zamorin of Calicut for three short years,from 1655-1658. Unlike the Zamorins who were known for their exploits on the battlefield, Manavedan is known for his single-minded devotion to Lord Guruvayurappan and Krishnagiti is an outpouring of that devotion.

Manavedan lived in a period of Vaishnava renaissance. Such periods invariably witness not only an upsurge in religious thought and practice but an accompanying renaissance in arts, music, dance and painting. This was the case all over India where devotion to Krishna was expressed through several art forms. "In Assam, Sankaradeva created the Sattriya dance-drama in the setting of the sattras or monastery-temples to be practiced by monks as an expression of Krishnabhakti. In Navadwip in Bengal, Sri Chaitanya Mahaprabhu was the progenitor of the soul stirring Sankirtana music and ecstatic dance. In Tamil Nadu Sri Narayana Teertha composed the Krishna Leela Tarangini in Sanskrit, inspired by Jayadeva's Gita Govinda, based on the life and leelas of Sri Krishna. These songs are danced to, to this day. Krishnanattam too was among these art forms and one nurtured by the patronage of the Zamorins." (Vedanta Kesari)

The story is that once Manavedan was in Guruvayur along with Vilwamangalam Swamiyar. Vilwamangalam was a great yogi, such an ardent devotee that he could see Bhagavan Krishna's enchanting form whenever he wished. Manavedan once beseeched Vilwamangalam to help him have the darshan of Krishna as well. Swamiyar replied that he needed to seek Bhagavan's permission. Accordingly, the next day he informed Manavedan that Bhagavan had agreed and that he would be able to have his darshan playing under the Ilanji (Mimusops elengi or Bakula) tree. To his great delight, Manavedan was able to see little Krishna playing under the tree scooping sand into coconut shells. Manavedan rushed to embrace the beautiful form of Bhagavan when He disappeared saying, "But Vilwamangalam did not mention a hug!" Manavedan got a peacock feather from Lord Krishna's headgear.. He rushed into the sanctum and pledged that he would design a headgear with that peacock feather, compose a dance drama and dedicate it to Krishna. The Ilanji tree stood at the site where the present Koothambalam (temple-theatre) stands, to the southeast of the sanctum. An idol of Sri Krishna was fashioned from the wood of that very tree and Manavedan began to worship the idol. He sat before the idol and composed the Krishnageeti in eight cantos, designed the headgear, the costumes and the facial make-up. He completed the choreography and decided on the music and instruments to be used.. A crown was fashioned with a feather as part of it. The story is that this was used as the first ever Krishnamudi, or crown in Krishnanattam." (Bards of Guruvayur, Vedanta Kesari)

The Krishnageeti is based on the 10th and 11th cantos of the Bhagavata Purana, inspired by Jayadeva's GitaGovinda, Melputhur's Narayaneeyam and Srikrishnavilasam Mahakavyam. Incidents from Sri Krishna's life are presented in eight parts: Avataram, Kaliyamardanam, Rasakreeda, Kamsavadham, Swayamvaram, Banayuddham, Vividhavadham and Swargarohanam. Avataram was re-enacted on the ninth day as Manavedan thought it inauspicious to end the series with Lord Krishna's demise. The practice has continued to this day.

As an art form, Krishnattam is in many ways the precursor to Kathakali where performance, music vocal and instrumental, choreography, hand (musts) and facial gestures are all synchronised to tell a story.together to express ideas."It draws generously on Ashtapadiyattam, early earthy dance forms like Theyyattam, Thirayattam, Mudiyettu and more importantly, on the Sanskrit theatre that survived in Kerala as Koodiyattam. In the Krishnageeti, Manavedan mentions the raga and tala to be followed for each song. The music is close to the sopana style of rendering ashtapadis. Krishnanattam, as we see it today, combines the soft and graceful feminine lasya with the vigorous tandava.

The costumes, facial makeup and mudras in Krishnattam have largely been influenced by Koodiyattam. Sanskrit is the medium for music in both Koodiyattam and Krishnagiti are in Sanskrit, but in Koodiyattam, the actors themselves recite slokas, while in Krishnattam they are sung to set ragas and thalas by expert musicians in the background. The percussion instrument in Koodiyattam is Mizhavu, while in Krishnattam there are two maddalams in the background, the Sudha Maddalam and the Thoppi Maddalam. While Krishnattam has adopted some dances from Koodiyattam, it has developed many new, beautiful dances to suit its own needs. As Zamorins P K S Raja noted in his article on Manavedan " in Krishnattam, much more importance is paid to the dances than to the background music. In Avatharam and Rasakrida, there is an exquisite piece of dance called Mullappoo Chuttal which is worth miles to go and see. Though in Krishnattam, lasya type of dance (slow rhythmic dance) is given prominence, the other types are not neglected. For example, the Thandava type of dance performed by the Mallas in Kamsavadham and by Murasura and Narakasura in Banayudham are perfect in style and rhythm. The Elakiyattam (mostly depicting anger) by Kamsa in Avatharam, Yavana and Rukmi in Swayamvarom and Sisupala in Vividavadham are brilliant pieces of dances."

Manavedan was Zamorins for only three years.. Zamorins normally lived in Kozhikode but Manavedan insisted on staying at Guruvayur and built a palace and moved his administrative office to Guruvayur.

It is believed that Manavedan died in 1658 in Thrissur while preparing for a war with the Dutch. His body was brought to Guruvayur and cremated in a corner of the palace.

The palace was later acquired by the Guruvayur Devaswom and in its place a Rest House
(Kaustubham) was erected. In the corner where Manavedan's body was cremated, the Devaswom has put up a statue of Manavedan, the great devotee.

There is a great paucity of material on Manavedan Raja. Among available records is an excellent article by Zamorins P K S Raja (Zamorin August 2003 to March 2013)- Krishnattam and Manavedan Raja, published in 2004.

There is also an exhaustive narrative: Bards of Guruvayur: Manavedan Raja- published in Vedanta Kesari, A Spiritual English Monthly of the Ramakrishna Order.August 2022 published by the Ramakrishna

VI

KURURAMMA

Yet another contemporary of Melpthur and Poonthanam was Kururamma, (1570-1640)who too belonged to a Nambudiri family. Her name was Gauri, referred to as Gauri Antharjanamo Purayannur Mana when she was brought to Kurkure as a young bride. She had married into the Kurur family in Adathu village near Thrissur and as the eldest member of the Kurur family came to be known as Kururamma. Kururamma lost her husband at the age of sixteen. She had no children. Her inner sense of loneliness made her realise that she had none to look forward to but Guruvayurappan. She became an ardent devotee and her Bhakti raised her to high spiritual heights.

In her dreams, Kururamma started seeing Lord Krishna and in one of them Krishna asked what boon she would like to have. She replied that she was lonely and would like Krishna to come as her son . Sometime later, an orphan came to her and and started staying with her. She called him Unni and used to play with him, even scolding him when he was naughty and was immensely fond of him. Not realising it was Lord Krishna who was invisible to other members of the family.

There are several stories about the miraculous events surrounding Kururamma.

It was said another devotee, Chemmanggat Amma was jealous of the growing fame of Kururamma. Chemmanggat Amma took great pride in Vilvamanagalath Swamiyar coming to her house for alms. In turn, Kururamma declared that the Swamiyar would come to her house next as a bhikshu. She invited him but the Swamiyar refused saying that he had to go for alms to Chemmanggat.

As was the custom, one person blew a conch before the Swaminarayan went for alms. As the Swami proceeded, the conch blower tried but could not produce any sound. The Swami then thought of his refusal to go to Kururamma and of her devotion for Guruvayurappan. He immediately started moving towards Kururamma's house. The conch started blowing once again.

It was said that Vilvamangalath Swamiyar could see the Lord in several forms and even converse with him. In Kururamma's house, Vilvamangalam once went to do the Pooja. As he started chanting the mantras and showering flowers, he noticed that the flowers were all falling at the feet of a little boy standing in front of him, the boy Unni who was staying with Kururamma. Annoyed with this, his sishyas asked the boy to stand away in a corner. The flowers continued to fall at the feet of the boy. Intrigued the Swamiyar meditated and realised that the boy was indeed Lord Krishna.

There is also the story of a Brahmin who had acute stomach pain and approached Vilvamangalath Swamiyar for help. The Swami replied that the pain was the result of several sins committed by the Brahmin in past lives and that there was no cure for it in this life or birth. The Brahmin went to Kururamma who offered him food. The Brahmin was hungry but could not eat because of stomach pain.

Kururamma asked him to do Krishna japa always and come to her house for his meal. He was soon miraculously cured of his stomach ache.

The Kurur illlam is located at Velur, Vengilassery area of Thalpilly Taluk .it is close to the Thrissur- Kunnamkulam highway. At this site now stands the Kururamma Sri Krishna Temple where the presiding deity is Krishna as Balagopala.

Large numbers of devotees visit this temple seeking the fulfilment of their wishes. The annual Prathishta day is celebrated on a grand scale.

Source: Kururamma – Krishna Devotee From Kerala Who Adopted Krishna As Her Child
By Abhilash Rajendran Sunday, January 26, 2020, In HINDU BLOG

VII
Chembai Vaidyanatha Bhagavathar

The life of Chembai Vaidyanatha Bhagavathar(1896 to 1974) is a modern day tale of the spiritual experience an ardent devotee goes through.

Coming from a family with a tradition of learning and teaching Carnatic music for over four generations, Chembai began showing early signs of his genius and creativity. He learnt Carnatic music from his father Ananta Bhagavathar and had his first public performance at the age of nine and his concert at Guruvayur at the age of eleven.

There is an interesting story about Chem bai's first concert at Guruvayur. Chembai (at 11), and his brother first sang at the Sree Krishna temple in Guruvayur on the Ekadashi day.As they came out of the temple, a policemen came up and said the inspector would like them to accompany him to the police station. Chembai's father was nonplussed by this and wondered what they had done to receive a call from the police. On reaching the police station, the Inspector received them with warmth and affection and said to the father, "Your boy must sing here on Sunday". That Sunday Chembai gave a concert and received 115 rupees, the highest paid for a concert. As advised by his father, Chembai kept the money received for worship at the temple.

In addition to vocal music, Chembai began to be trained in violin and flute. He used this to gain entry as a violinist into a music concert by an established Carnatic vocalist of the time. After the concert he insisted on singing a couple of famous Kritis. The organiser, himself a giant among musicians of the time, was so impressed that he encouraged the young lad to continue enthralling the audience!

Between 1912 and 1927 Chembai sang at several music sabhas and festivals including those organised by the Music Academy in Chennai. He earned a name for his virtuosity. Chembai's voice had a grandeur of its own; it was noted for its metallic timbre, rich melody, resonance and vigorous style. Ragas shone in his voice with solid classicism. His style was one free of frills and unwanted decorations. Together with Ariyakudi Ramanuja Ayyangar and Maharajapuram Vishwanatha Iyer, Chembai formed the trinity of the Carnatic music of his period. He soon started receiving several accolades including the Ganagandharva Award in 1940 from Kalki Krishnamurty and the coveted Sangeeta Kalanidhi from the Music Academy in 1951.

Chembai's concerts invariably ended with the recital of a shloka from the 100th dashakam of Narayaneeyam. Recordings of his recitals of 'Agre pasyami' and 'Yogeendranam' are available on YouTube.

It was said that at a concert in Shichindram, Chembai lost his voice. He could not chant the names of Lord Guruvayurappan. He prayed fervently. Almost miraculously a stranger appeared and offered to treat him for eighteen days. This was done in Poomallianmana at the residence of Neelakantan Nambudirippad. This worked and Chem bai's voice was restored with increased vigour. Since then he has donated a major portion of his earnings to the Guruvayur temple.

On 16 October 1974 Chembai gave a concert at Poozhikunnu Sreekrishna temple at Ottappalam, where he had coincidentally given his first concert. He ended the concert, as he often did, with the rendition of the song, " Karuna Cheiyvan enthu thamasam Krishna".(Why this delay in conferring your mercy on me, Krishna). He then talked to his disciple and returned to Olappamanna Vasudevan NAMBUDIRI's residence where he used to spend a day or two whenever he visited Ottappalam. He washed his feet and face and sat down for prayers. Soon one of the members present, noticing that his head was sliding to one side rushed and supported his body. Olappamanna who was a seasoned observer of ' Marana lakshanas' (death signs) came to examine him. It took him a few seconds to say ' it is all over'.

Chembai's nephew had once said that Chembai had often wished for an easy death.

He could not have expected a better boon from Lord Guruvayurappan.

Post script

Chembai had been conducting a music festival at his village every year. This has been continued by his family and is known as the Chembai Ekadasi Festival.Chembai also held every year a music concert at Guruvayur on Guruvayur

Ekadasi day, in November. This is now a music festival, Chembai Sangeetotsavam conducted by the Guruvayur Devaswom Board and is spread over two weeks. Several leading artistes perform at this festival every year and many newcomers get an opportunity to showcase their talents.

VIII

Guruvayur Kesavan

One might wonder whether the story of Guruvayur Kesavan is one from the Puranas or whether we are recreating a story based on wish more than reality. Like Gajendramoksham, is this a story of a devotee who had to take the form of an elephant in this birth as penance for something he did or did not do? The story of Kesavan is the story of an elephant that was predestined to live with and love Guruvayurappan, of an elephant that, but for its lack of human form, behaved with the same devotion to the Lord as the human devotee did. That elephants have a high level of intelligence, both conventional and emotional, has been proved through both research and experience of those who have had to deal with them. They understand languages, They communicate amongst themselves, and they express joy, grief ,anger and love. They are immensely attached to their loved ones.

Here was an elephant that would take a round (pradaksinam) of the temple every time he returned from a trip. Here was one who would bow before the Lord without being instructed to do so. Here was an elephant full of compassion even in its wildest moods and would show it profusely to the needy.

There is the story of Kesvan letting himself loose of the mahouts and running round the temple once. The devotees, frightened of Kesvan's mood, started running for safety. One person alone, disabled and suffering from leprosy remained in the middle, unable to move. He looked at Kesavan and the elephant, however mad he may have been with what one could not have guessed, stopped suddenly, lifted him with his trunks delicately and placed him delicately in a place close by before he started again his rounds.

Kesavan was one of the twelve elephants that the Senior of Nailambur had in 1920s. Once in dire anguish, to be saved from his foes, the Raja prayed to Guruvayurappan and vowed that, should he be rescued from his enemies, he would donate one of his elephants to Guruvayurappan. His wish was granted, The result was the donation of Kesvan to Guruvayurappan. This was on.4th January 1922.

From then till his death on 2nd December 1976 Kesavn spent his days in the service of Guruvayurappan.

Kesavan was a tall elephant but would not be rated as the most stately elephant in a group of contemporaries who were a company to him in a temple utsavam. (The practice in the 1920s and 30's was to have ten or twelve elephants in an utsavam and give the honour of carrying the Thidambu (the decorated replica of the deity in a temple that is usually taken outside for the purposes like festivals and poojas) to the tallest and most stately one. It was said that when Kesavan carried the thidambu he had an altogether different personality, he looked a king among men with an extra inch height! Kesavan would also not tolerate the honour of carrying the thidambu being given to any other elephant. He would kick up a ruckus. This has happened on a few occasions. Perhaps for this reason he was referred to as the mad elephant. In my own childhood, I have heard of Kesavan doing this in the utsavam at the Shiva temple in Kottakkal. He ran riot completely spoiling the show and disrupting the proceedings because he was apparently not given the honour of being the leader . That created a big scare among both the performers, spectators and even elephants who ran for their safety. Three nambudiris were sitting on Kesavan's back. In the midst of the disorder that ensued and lasted for over an hour none was attacked by Kesavan and no injuries were reported.

There are other stories of Kesavan's love and devotion. It was said that Kesavan would show his front leg for the priest to climb only if the thidambu were to be lifted and be carried by him. All others will have to climb up via his hind leg! Kesavan was also noted for certain things he did on his own: whenever he retuned from a trip he would immediately go inside the temple, take a round (pradakshinam) and bow before the Lord.

Guruvayur Kesavan lived for more than fifty years in the service of the
Lord. His fame had spread throughout Kerala and he was in great demand for temple festivals. In 1973, celebrating his golden jubilee of service to the temple, the temple authorities conferred on him the title "Gajarajan", something no other elephant had received.

In December 1976, on the auspicious Ekadasi day,Kesavan fell sick during the time of the procession inside the temple. He was withdrawn from the procession into a stable close by. There he lay and fasted throughout the night. The next evening when the conch blew to announce the appearance of the Deity, Kesavan bowed and shortly after, he collapsed and died.

A memorial to Kesavan in the form of a 12 ft concrete statue stands in front of the Panchajanyam guest house in Kizhakke Nada. Kesa van's tusks and portrait are displayed at the entrance to the inner chamber of the temple. Tributes to Guruvayur Kesavan have come in other forms, in the form of articles, a movie and pranams from devotees.

One might wonder whether the story of Guruvayur Kesavan is one from the Puranas or whether we are recreating a story based on wish more than reality. Like Gajendramoksham, is this a story of a devotee who had to take the form of an elephant in this birth as penance for something he did or did not do? The story of Kesavan is the story of an elephant that was predestined to live with and love Guruvayurappan, of an elephant that, but for its lack of human form, behaved with the same devotion to the Lord as the human devotee did. That elephants have a high level of intelligence, both conventional and emotional, has been proved through both research and experience of those who have had to deal with them. They understand languages, They communicate amongst themselves, and they express joy, grief ,anger and love. They are immensely attached to their loved ones.

Here was an elephant that would take a round (pradaksinam) of the temple every time he returned from a trip. Here was one who would bow before the Lord without being instructed to do so. Here was an elephant full of compassion even in its wildest moods and would show it profusely to the needy.

There is the story of Kesvan letting himself loose of the mahouts and running round the temple once. The devotees, frightened of Kesvan's mood, started running for safety. One person alone, disabled and suffering from leprosy remained in the middle, unable to move. He looked at

Kesavan and the elephant, however mad he may have been with what one could not have guessed, stopped suddenly, lifted him with his trunks delicately and placed him delicately in a place close by before he started again his rounds.

Kesavan was one of the twelve elephants that the Senior of Nailambur had in 1920s. Once in dire anguish, to be saved from his foes, the Raja prayed to Guruvayurappan and vowed that, should he be rescued from his enemies, he would donate one of his elephants to Guruvayurappan. His wish was granted, The result was the donation of Kesvan to Guruvayurappan. This was on.4th January 1922.

From then till his death on 2nd December 1976 Kesavn spent his days in the service of Guruvayurappan.

Kesavan was a tall elephant but would not be rated as the most stately elephant in a group of contemporaries who were a company to him in a temple utsavam. (The practice in the 1920s and 30's was to have ten or twelve elephants in an utsavam and give the honour of carrying the Thidambu (the decorated replica of the deity in a temple that is usually taken outside for the purposes like festivals and poojas) to the tallest and most stately one. It was said that when Kesavan carried the thidambu he had an altogether different personality, he looked a king among men with an extra inch height! Kesavan would also not tolerate the honour of carrying the thidambu being given to any other elephant. He would kick up a ruckus. This has happened on a few occasions. Perhaps for this reason he was referred to as the mad elephant. In my own childhood, I have heard of Kesavan doing this in the utsavam at the Shiva temple in Kottakkal. He ran riot completely spoiling the show and disrupting the proceedings because he was apparently not given the honour of being the leader . That created a big scare among both the performers, spectators and even elephants who ran for their safety. Three nambudiris were sitting on Kesavan's back. In the midst of the disorder that ensued and lasted for over an hour none was attacked by Kesavan and no injuries were reported.

There are other stories of Kesavan's love and devotion. It was said that Kesavan would show his front leg for the priest to climb only if the thidambu were to be lifted and be carried by him. All others will have to climb up via his hind leg! Kesavan was also noted for certain things he did on his own: whenever he retuned from a trip he would immediately go inside the temple, take a round (pradakshinam) and bow before the Lord.

Guruvayur Kesavan lived for more than fifty years in the service of the
Lord. His fame had spread throughout Kerala and he was in great demand for temple festivals. In 1973, celebrating his golden jubilee of service to the temple, the temple authorities conferred on him the title "Gajarajan", something no other elephant had received.

In December 1976, on the auspicious Ekadasi day,Kesavan fell sick during the time of the procession inside the temple. He was withdrawn from the procession into a stable close by. There he lay and fasted throughout the night. The next evening when the conch blew to announce the appearance of the Deity, Kesavan bowed and shortly after, he collapsed and died.

A memorial to Kesavan in the form of a 12 ft concrete statue stands in front of the Panchajanyam guest house in Kizhakke Nada. Kesa van's tusks and portrait are displayed at the entrance to the inner chamber of the temple. Tributes to Guruvayur Kesavan have come in other forms, in the form of articles, a movie and pranams from devotees.

IX

Epilogue

The accounts given in the foregoing are merely illustrative. They do not uncover similar experiences that hundreds of devotees who flock to Guruvayur may have had. Guruvayur is the third largest temple in the country in terms of the number of visitors. It is estimated that more than 6 million devotees come to the temple every year and that the number has kept on increasing as people from other parts of the country have known of the power of the deity and of the experiences of the visiting devotees. There are now replicas of the Guruvayur temple in many parts of India and even abroad. Here the visitor sees the ever-shining image of the Lord. These temples receive vazhivadu in the same manner as the main temple at Guruvayur does.

For more than four centuries now, Guruvayur has been in the public consciousness. There has been a qualitative change in the way Guruvayur conducts itself. Over the last thirty years or so there has been a qualitative change in the way Guruvayur organises its life and workflow: accessibility with the rail connection and widening of roads; distinct improvement in sanitation and cleanliness all around; better lodging facilities ; a more organised flow of traffic inside the temple, even though devotees still have to hurry through their darshan; and planning of annual events with a calendar published well in advance. It is believed that the Central Government is engaged in developing a master plan for the development of Guruvayur as a temple city, a place of worship where much larger numbers of devotees can come in and fall at the feet of the Lord. That would be a fitting tribute to the glory of Guruvayurappan.

Ingram Content Group UK Ltd.
Milton Keynes UK
UKHW040928190523
422019UK00001B/8